<$The Canadian Authorpreneuer's Tax Journal$>

2019-2020-2021>

by <$Laurie Stewart$>

ISBN: 978-1-988688-42-8

Foreword

How to use this book

This book deals with Canadian taxes only. Sorry, but I am only familiar with the taxes in my own country. While many things in here also apply to other countries, you will need to confirm tax rates, what can be claimed, etc. for your particular country. If you sell books worldwide, you may be required to submit tax returns in those countries as well, though most have a treaty with Canada that ensures that you will not be double taxed on your income. Amazon, Draft2Digital, and Ingraham-

Spark.com both allow you to select a tax rate of 0% if you do not live in the States.

I use the term Authorpreneur because as a self-published or hybrid author, there is a need for you to be an entrepreneur-business person as well as an artist. This applies to artistpreneurs, too.

This book will explain a bit about how taxes for artists work, what you can claim, what you need to keep records of, etc. It has examples, and a place to write down expenses and income, and has monthly calendars, to-do lists, and space for your own notes.

At the time of writing, exact amounts for personal deductions, taxation and marginal tax rates, etc for 2020 were not available. The will be available on www.cra-arc.gc.ca in February 2020. You can also call 1-800-959-5525 and ask a real, live person. Eventually.

I have therefore used 2019 figures, which should not be too far off, and good for estimating your tax load.

Gifi codes and Capital Cost Allowance amounts rarely change, so those figures are good to go.

I also have a section on my website (www.lauriestewart-author.com) for authorpreneurship, and will update figures and rules as CRA releases them. I am available for 1 on 1 coaching by appointment at cons or in Ottawa. Watch my blog to see where I'll be. You can contact me through my website or on Facebook at Laurie Stewart: Writer, Film-maker, Painter.

Index:

The Nitty-gritty

Different Taxes

HST, Corp. Tax and Personal Tax

GST/HST:

If you are registered for GST/HST, you must collect it on all income. Or include it in the price of the book, workshop, etc and calculate how much is tax when you file at the end of the year (Sale price/1.13 = basic price, Deduct basic price from Sale price to get HST)

3.99(sale price) /1.13 = $3.50

$3.99 - $3.53 = $.46 HST

GST/HST Form:

You claim all of the GST/HST you pay on everything related to your business as an input tax credit on line 101. So all of the tax on computers, gas, desks, food(50%), printer paper, etc. If you are in a province that does not have the Harmonized Sales Tax, you can only claim the GST portion, not the PST.

You also claim all of the GST/HST you collected from sales on line 106.

There is an adjustment line for the GST/HST you claimed on a bad debt from a previous year. This prevents you from paying taxes on income you never received.

Deduct the tax you paid from the tax you collected. If you paid out more than you collected, which is very likely in your first few years, you will get the difference back. This is why I recommend registering for the GST/HST before you start selling or making money.

In my first year, I sold like 6 books, mostly to family, I should not have released in late Oct. But I bought a laptop, a tablet, a printer... I got my HST back. All of it.

Corporate Tax:

Federal tax on a corporation earning under $500,000 / year is considered a small business. These are the rates you would use on the left. On the right are the "active business" or larger corporations.

	Small Business Income		Active Business Income[3]	
	2018	2019 and Beyond	2018	2019 and Beyond
Federal rates				
General corporate rate	38.0%	38.0%	38.0%	38.0%
Federal abatement	(10.0) 28.0	(10.0) 28.0	(10.0) 28.0	(10.0) 28.0
Small business deduction[4]	(18.0)	(19.0)	0.0	0.0
Rate reduction[5]	0.0	0.0	(13.0)	(13.0)
	10.0	9.0	15.0	15.0
Provincial rates				
British Columbia[6]	2.0%	2.0%	12.0%	12.0%
Alberta	2.0	2.0	12.0	12.0
Saskatchewan[7]	2.0	2.0	12.0	12.0
Manitoba[8]	0.0	0.0	12.0	12.0
Ontario[9]	3.5	3.5	11.5	11.5
Quebec[10]	8.0	8.0	11.7	11.6/11.5
New Brunswick[11]	3.0/2.5	2.5	14.0	14.0
Nova Scotia	3.0	3.0	16.0	16.0
Prince Edward Island[12]	4.0	4.0	16.0	16.0
Newfoundland and Labrador	3.0	3.0	15.0	15.0

The rates (as of June 30, 2019) will remain the same for 2020.

In most provinces you do only the federal return and send your cheque (if you're paying taxes) to CRA and they deal with the provincial filing and send them a cheque for their share. In Quebec and Alberta, you need to do separate returns. More work, but same amount of taxes paid.

If, as is normal for beginners, you lose money from setting up and working and networking, without ANY sales... you can carry your loss forward up to 20 years, until you start making money. You then claim these losses to reduce your tax position back to zero.

CRA will allow you to not make any sales for 4 years before they start to question whether you are indeed trying to make a living. Remember the "reasonable expectation of profit"? If you have been taking workshops, meeting people, have a writers group, etc. then you are fine, because this shows that you are trying.

Personal Tax: Federal tax starts at about 23% and On tax is 5.05% for a total of 28.5%. If you have a really good day job, you could be taxed as high as 53%. Thus it is beneficial to separate yourself from your imprint and leave as much money as possible in the company.

If you decide to go as an individual (Form T2125) rather than incorporating, everything will be added together under income on line 150 of your T-1. You will not need a balance sheet, but you will still need a statement of income and loss to show where the money went. It is attached to Form T2125.

Also, you cannot carry a loss forward for as long or carry back as far. In any tax year, you first must reduce your taxes owing to zero before carrying the remaining loss. Good news, you can use writing losses to reduce the tax paid by your day job.

However, Use of Home expenses cannot be carried forward under either Corporate or Personal, so use them to reduce your tax load to zero. Then carry the actual expenses to a year with profits.

This is why most incorporate the publishing wing, and use their writing expenses to lower their personal taxes.

Getting Organized

SAVE EVERY RECEIPT!

Decide later if you can claim it, this gets you out of the habit of tossing receipts away.

Put them in the same place every time. I used to have a pretty red box by the door and all receipts go in there until I can sort them.

Keep a special drawer full of 8X11 envelopes for your receipts. One of those cute Dollar Store accordion receipt thingies will never be big enough. Though the big office supply ones might.

Make a spreadsheet to track sales by book title on one page, and by month on another. If you combine these, you will still need to track book by platform; ebook or physical.

*Unless you are really good at spreadsheets, do not attempt to combine everything on one page, you'll get a brain aneurism.

Use GIFI codes on your envelopes, this will save a lot of time later. Ie: Office supplies (paper, notebooks, pens, stamps)-8811

Save all household bills including repairs, you'll need them for use of home expenses.

Write what a receipt is for on the receipt as soon as you get it.

Write mileage at beginning and end of business trips in your notebook, keep a page just for this, you'll need it to calculate use of car expenses.

Print royalty statements as soon as you receive them to file. Keep folders in your email for receipts, royalties, contracts.

INCOME					
Royalty By Platform	**Physical/ Ebook**	**Jan**	**Feb**	**Mar**	**Apr**
Amazon	Ebook	150			
Amazon	Physical	35			
KU	Pages	701			
Draft2Digital	Ebook	450			
Smashwords	Ebook	36			
Ingraham-Spark	Physical	190			
Corvid Moon	Physical	250			
Corvid Moon	Ebook	169			
Sold in person	Physical	155			
BY Book Title	**Royalty/ Advance**	**Jan**	**Feb**	**Mar**	**Apr**
Title 4	Advance	500			
Title 1	Royalty	26			
Title 2	Royalty	38			

Record Keeping

You will need at least a dozen file folders or large envelopes.

You must save receipts if you want to claim it, no proof means no deduction. Keep the receipts for 7 years, in case CRA wants to review them.

Don't panic if you lose some or if CRA denies them. All that will happen is that you must pay the tax on the disallowed deduction. But don't waste time about it. A cranky auditor = more problems and stress than necessary.

Keep detailed records of conferences/ conventions you attend. These are networking events and much of it can be written off. Especially if you get a meeting with an agent, editor, publisher, etc.

Keep track of your GST/HST on every receipt.

Books on history, fashion, science, writing styles, how-to books, etc. are research materials. So are trips to museums for specific exhibits, like the Viking exhibit in Ottawa in 2015.

Books or magazines by a publisher you intend to pitch to can be seen as research. If you claim them, be prepared to defend the deduction. It helps if you claim only books in your genre, research into specific eras or events, and have a pitch letter or a meeting to show for it.

Claim your professional memberships! Canadian Authors Assoc., local writers organizations, Ad Astra membership, Science Fiction and Fantasy Assoc., Romance Writers Assoc., Etc.

Filing Taxes

On Form T2125: Personal Business

As a self-employed individual, you may have to make instalment payments.

Instalment payments are due on;

March 15

June 15

September 15, and

December 15.

You will need to check with CRA to see if this applies to you, it usually depends on income. You will be charged penalties and interest if you are supposed to file instalments and don't.

Annual GST/HST returns for the previous year are due by April 15th, and your T-1 tax return on April 30th. Your Business return (T-2) is due on June 30th. It's best to file them the same day so you don't forget.

You will need to fill out Form T2125 as well as a statement of Income and Loss, and a detailed sheet of income and expenses. These will be tucked into your T-1 and submitted with it. So will several other forms and schedules.

You will need to insert the income/ loss numbers from T2125 onto the appropriate pages of your T-1, under Business Gross (line 162) and Net (line 135) on page 2.

You must file and pay CPP deductions on your writing income (schedule 8) but it's in your favour. This adds to the amount of old age pension you will receive.

From the CRA website:

" Self-employed persons

- Send your CPP contributions to when you file yourT1 income tax and benefit return.
- Your contributions are based on net business income.
- When you do your taxes, separate your CPP contributions into two parts: CPP base contributions and CPP enhanced contributions. The base contribution is the amount that is calculated at a rate of 9.9% (which you currently contribute in 2019), and the enhanced portion is

the amount above that, the new rate is 10.2%. Currently, you can claim a 15% non-refundable tax credit on 4.95% of the base CPP contributions and claim a tax deduction on the other 4.95%. You will continue to do this after the enhancement. You will also claim a tax deduction on the enhanced portion of your contributions.

(Example: You pay a total of $6120 CPP in 2019. The base rate would be (9.9%) is $5940. 4.95% of $5940 = $294.03 of which you can claim 15%. Plus you can claim the other $294.03 as business tax deduction.)

- **Electronic filers**– If you file your return electronically using commercial tax software that is certified for NETFILE, or a tax preparer completes and files your return using EFILE, the tax software will perform all of the necessary calculations. It will automatically separate and apply the base and enhanced contributions for you.
- **Paper filers**– Schedule 8, CPP Contributions on Self-Employment and Other Earnings, will break down your base and enhanced amounts. A new line (Line 223) will be added to

your T1 return where you will enter the enhanced amount of your contributions from Schedule 8. The CPP base amount will be entered on line 308, as in the past.

- The CRA's payroll deduction tables and formulas will be updated to present the base CPP and the enhancement as one combined deduction for each pay period.

- Amended T4127 payroll deduction formulas, taking effect January 1, 2019, will be available on November 15, 2018. Amended T4032 and T4008 payroll deduction tables and supplementary tables will be available December 15, 2018. SeePayroll Deductions Online Calculator (PDOC), payroll tables, TD1s, and more. https://www.canada.ca/en/revenue-agency/services/e-services/e-services-businesses/payroll-deductions-online-calculator.html"

You will also claim the CPP amount on Page 3, line 222.

On Form T2125, part 4 you will be asked to calculate the cost of goods sold. This is the costs of editing, designing, covers, printing, shipping to you from printer, customs duty, etc., to figure out the cost of each book you sell. Ebooks are deducted as a lump sum, physical books are deducted on the amount sold only.

This cost of goods sold is calculated every year, each year's opening inventory must equal the previous year's closing.

Business "use of home" is calculated in part 8, and inserted onto line 61 in part 6. Capital Cost Allowance is calculated in part 11 and inserted at line 52 in part 6. "Use of car" expenses are calculated in part 17, and inserted at line 50 in part 6.

When in doubt, call 1-800-959-5525 (corporate) or 1-800-959-8281 (personal) and ask.

On Form T-2: As a corporation

This is the return for your business only, you must still file a T-1 for your personal taxes.

You must have an assigned Business Number for this. Simply fill out the registration info at Industry Canada's website and you'll automatically get one. The good news is that all your tax numbers will be the same, only the suffixes change. RC0001 for Corporate tax, RT0001 for HST payments, etc.

*If you can navigate the paperwork yourself, it will cost $200 to incorporate federally, $20 for a name search (mandatory) and /or $60 just to register your own name as a business (not incorporated)

Or you can pay me $400+ for me to do it.

Schedule 1 must be filled out and will give you most of the numbers you need.

While a large amount of the T-2 is geared toward larger businesses, it may be worth filling out the various schedules just to see if you qualify. Each one has a different income/ employee level to qualify for tax deductions.

You can then figure out whether you can use the short form T-2, which is MUCH simpler.

In your first year, you should also try calculating your HST/GST with both the "Quick Method" (http://www.cra-arc.gc.ca/E/pub/gp/rc4058/rc4058-e.html#P100_5211) and the write down every purchase and count it up method. You may find that one results in a bigger refund than the other. Though the quick method is more confusing the first time you use it.

Your cheque for taxes owed should accompany your return.

What Can I Claim

What can I claim? And how?

You can claim anything related to running your business. Some things you may need to answer questions about, as they are unique expenses for writers or artists.

This includes such things as art supplies, research books, bookmarks, postcards, conventions and conferences, sending books to the Library and Archives in Ottawa, and more.

Some items you may need to discuss with an auditor if they disallow a deduction. Items they usually flag (but can be defended):

Working vacation days. If you have meetings with editors or agents, etc., while on vacation, or if you are appearing at a con and extend your visit; you may claim a percentage of your travel, accommodations and meals. ie: 2 days with meetings on a 1 week vacation = 2/7 of expenses are claimable. Remember that you would claim 50% of your meals only on those two days.

You can claim 100% of con fees, parking, travel, accommodations and 50% of meals, while you are at a conference/ convention, and while networking or meeting with authors, editors, agents, etc. HOWEVER, they now allow only 2 cons/year. So my advice is to A) claim the most expensive 2 as it includes airfare and accommodations. Use this to try to lower your taxes on your day-job to $0. B) Claim 2 others (the next most expensive) as your imprint/ corporation if you set one up.

If you write a specific genre, you can claim books, museum visits and DVDs as research IN THAT GENRE. It is best to have a pitch letter or meeting with a publisher, agent or editor in that genre as proof that it was research.

NOTE: if you are incorporated, or registered for GST/HST, you will need to claim the tax on your GST/HST return and the pre-tax total in your business deductions.

While on vacation, if you are researching a location; you can claim park or festival fees, parking at specific events, hotel and travel (see above)

These can all be claimed on a separate spreadsheet for Writing Expenses, and then added into your business expenses on a T2125 or your T-2.

If you are disabled and need help on a daily basis with your wheelchair, driving, luggage, etc; you can claim your assistant's expenses (including pay if applicable) The assistant's meals are 100% because they are a business expense.

Example: I am mobility impaired. While I can walk short distances without pain, I use a wheelchair at cons. Because hotels use thick rugs for comfortable walking, it's difficult to push my chair. So I need a friend or my husband to attend just to push me around.

Since he is not attending the con for his own interests or professional development, I can deduct 100% of his con fee, meals, parking, plus include him in my travel and accommodations. Unless he needs his own room (normal for a hired assistant) where I can claim both rooms at 100%.

* GST/HST is tracked and reported separately.

Calendars:

October to November 2019

January to December 2020

January to March 2021

Oct-Nov 2019

Calendars and Notes

OCTOBER 2019

MON	TUES	WED	THUR	FRI	SAT	SUN
	1	2	3	4	5	6
7	8	9	10	11	12	13
14	15	16	17	18	19	20
21	*22*	23	24	25	26	27
28	*29*	30	31			

October 1st: Sort Sept's Receipts

October 14th: Thanksgiving

October 31st: Halloween/ Samhain

Notes:

NOVEMBER 2019

MON	TUES	WED	THUR	FRI	SAT	SUN
				1	2	
4	5	6	7	8	9	10
11	12	13	14	15	16	17
18	19	20	21	22	23	24
25	26	27	28	29	30	

November 1st: Sort October's Receipts

Nov 1st: All Souls Day

November 11th: Remembrance Day

Notes:

DECEMBER 2019

MON	TUES	WED	THUR	FRI	SAT	SUN
						1
2	3	4	5	6	7	8
9	10	11	12	13	14	15
16	17	18	19	20	21	22
23	24	25	26	27	28	29
30	31					

December 1st: Sort November's Receipts

December 21st: Winter Solstice

December 24th: Christmas Eve

December 25th: Christmas Day

December 26th: Boxing Day

Dec 31st: New Year's Eve

Notes:

JANUARY 2020

MON	TUES	WED	THUR	FRI	SAT	SUN
		1	2	3	4	5
6	7	8	9	10	11	12
13	14	15	16	17	18	9
20	21	22	23	24	25	26
27	28	29	30	31		

Jan 1st: New Year's Day

Jan 1st: write down car odometers.

Jan 3rd: Sort all December's Receipts

Start new envelopes and spreadsheet

Notes:

FEBRUARY 2020

MON	TUES	WED	THUR	FRI	SAT	SUN
					1	2
3	4	5	6	7	8	9
10	11	12	13	14	15	16
17	18	19	20	21	22	23
24	25	26	27	28		

February 1st: Sort January Receipts

February 14: Valentine's Day

February 26th: Ash Wednesday

Notes:

MARCH 2020

MON	TUES	WED	THUR	FRI	SAT	SUN
				1	2 1	1 2
3	4	5	6	7	8	9
10	11	12	13	14	15	16
17	18	19	20	21	22	23
24	25	26	27	28	29	30
31						

March 1st: Sort February Receipts

March 21st: Spring Equinox

Notes:

APRIL 2020

MON	TUES	WED	THUR	FRI	SAT	SUN
	1	2	3	4	5	6
7	8	9	10	11	12	13
14	15	16	17	18	19	20
21	22	23	24	25	26	27
28	29	30				

April 1st: Sort March Receipts

April 11th: Good Friday

April 12th: Easter

April 13th: Easter Sunday

April 14th: Easter Monday

April 30th: Beltaine

Notes:

MAY 2020

MON	TUES	WED	THUR	FRI	SAT	SUN
			1	2	3	4
5	6	7	8	9	10	11
12	13	14	15	16	17	18
19	20	22	23	24	25	26
27	28	29	30	31		

May 1st: Beltaine, May Day

Notes:

JUNE 2020

MON	TUES	WED	THUR	FRI	SAT	SUN
					1	2
3	4	5	6	7	8	9
10	11	12	13	14	15	16
17	18	19	20	21	22	23
24	25	26	27	28	29	30

June 1st: Sort May's Receipts

June 21st: Summer Solstice

Notes:

JULY 2020

MON	TUES	WED	THUR	FRI	SAT	SUN
1	2	3	4	5	6	7
8	9	10	11	12	13	14
15	16	17	18	19	20	21
22	23	24	25	26	27	28
29	30	31				

July 1st: Canada Day,

July 2nd: Sort June Receipts

Notes:

AUGUST 2020

MON	TUES	WED	THUR	FRI	SAT	SUN
			1	2	3	4
5	6	7	8	9	10	11
12	13	14	15	16	17	18
19	20	21	22	23	24	25
26	27	28	29	30	31	

Aug 1st: Sort July's Receipts

August 5th: Family Day

Notes:

SEPTEMBER 2020

MON	TUES	WED	THUR	FRI	SAT	SUN
						1
2	3	4	5	6	7	8
9	10	11	12	13	14	15
16	17	18	19	20	21	22
23	24	25	26	27	28	29
30						

September 1st: Sort August's Receipts

September 2nd: Labour Day,

September 21st: Fall Equinox

Notes:

OCTOBER 2020

MON	TUES	WED	THUR	FRI	SAT	SUN
	1	2	3	4	5	6
7	8	9	10	11	12	13
14	15	16	17	18	19	20
21	22	23	24	25	26	27
28	29	30	31			

October 1st: Sort September's Receipts

October 14th: Thanksgiving

October 31st Halloween, Samhain

Notes:

NOVEMBER 2020

MON	TUES	WED	THUR	FRI	SAT	SUN
				1	2	3
4	5	6	7	8	9	10
11	12	13	14	15	16	17
18	19	20	21	22	23	24
25	26	27	28	29	30	

November 1st: Sort October's Receipts

November 11th: Remembrance Day

Notes:

DECEMBER 2020

MON	TUES	WED	THUR	FRI	SAT	SUN
						1
2	3	4	5	6	7	8
9	10	11	12	13	14	**15**
16	17	**18**	**19**	**20**	21	22
23	24	25	26	27	28	29
30	31					

December 1st: Sort November's Receipts

December 21st: Winter Solstice

December 24th: Christmas Eve

December 25th: Christmas Day

December 26th: Boxing Day

December 31st: New Years Eve

Notes:

JANUARY 2021

MON	TUES	WED	THUR	FRI	SAT	SUN
		1	2	3	4	5
6	7	8	9	10	11	12
13	14	15	16	17	18	19
20	21	22	23	24	25	26
27	28	29	30	31		

January 1st: New Year's Day,

Sort December Receipts

Start new Files/ spreadsheet for 2021,

Write down Odometers

Notes:

FEBRUARY 2021

MON	TUES	WED	THUR	FRI	SAT	SUN
					1	2
3	4	5	6	7	8	9
10	11	12	13	14	15	16
17	18	19	20	21	22	23
24	25	26	24	28		

February 1st: Sort January's Receipts

February 14th: Valentine;s Day

Notes:

MARCH 2021

MON	TUES	WED	THUR	FRI	SAT	SUN
					1	2
3	4	5	6	7	8	9
10	11	12	13	14	15	16
17	18	19	20	21	22	23
24	25	26	27	28	29	30
31						

March 1st: Sort February's Receipts

March 22st: Spring Equinox

Notes:

Appendixes

Expenses, What can I claim?

Expenses are, in the simplest terms, what it costs to run a business. This includes a portion of your car and home if you use them for your business.

Typical expenses for a writer include:

Computer, printer, paper, notebooks, pens, ink/toner, cell phone, laptop/tablet, reference books, filing cabinet, writing programs, time management software, etc.

Printing costs including exchange rates, shipping taxes, duties. Ebook and audio covers formatted from print covers, formatting for different platforms (Kobo, Kindle, Sony, etc)

Tables and space rental for sales fairs, cons, etc.

Your writer's website.

Expenses you may not think of:

Library card, conventions as writer or reader, travel to cons or for research, hotels for cons or research, meals (50% of your meals) with a publisher, editor, beta-reader, writing group, etc. 100% of meals for a paid companion if you require one because of disability or a Personal Assistant, if you're needing one.

Furniture, cell or home phone if used mostly for business.

Money paid to: PA, sales assistant, cover artist, interior design, editors, formatters, audio recording, etc.

Basically everything you use for writing or publishing your own books.

If you are incorporated as a publisher, I use the expenses directly related to writing on my personal taxes, and any expenses related to printing, producing or selling books to my publishing arm.

I have a website for just my publishing, and one for each of my writing names.

GIFI Codes

What are they and where do they go?

General Index of Financial Information helps that everyone report the same expense in the same place or line. This makes it easier for tax departments, both Federal, provincial and international to compare apples to apples.

They are usually put in the far left column of a spreadsheet, and the same codes are used for the same items every year.

Looking them up on CRA's website may be confusing if you are looking for artist's codes. You are best to consider the broader descriptions. Like Sales and rental for sales of prints, photos, original artwork, and rental income for art shown in galleries, restaurants, etc.

Meals (9135) and Meals: working (8523) are different. Meals is at 50%, this is meals or drinks while networking, at cons, writing in a coffeeshop, etc.

Meals: Working is at 100% and this is food you provide to everyone at a meeting or event, or food eaten by an assistant if you are disabled.

If you are in doubt, claim 50% (9135) or consult a tax expert. Almost all meals will be in that category.

Inventory is only physical books on hand. Bookmarks, business cards, etc. are Office Exp. (8811) because they are given away, not sold

Writer's list of common GIFI codes

INCOME:	
Income Sales	8001
Income Royalties	8237
Income seminars/ coaching	8241

EXPENSES:	
Exp Accounting Fees	8862
Exp Advertising	8521
Exp Bank Charges	8715
Exp Books for Sale (buying from publisher)	8321
Exp Computer	9151
Exp Cons: Accommodation	9204
Exp Cons: Fees	9201

Exp Cons: Travel	9202
Exp contractors (editors, cover design, etc.)	8360
Exp Customs	8764
Exp Inventory Losses (stuff that was stolen or destroyed)	9273
Exp Legal Fees	8861
Exp Meals	9135
Exp Meals: working	8523
Exp Office expense	8811
Exp Postage for free copies	8810
Exp Printing	8814
Exp Professional Memberships	8761
Exp Promo: books given away, tables at sales, cons, fairs	8524
Exp Proofs	8320
Exp Research	9282
Exp Royalties to authors	9277
Exp Shipping	9275
Exp Software Updates	9151
Exp Training	8876

Exp Vehicle, gas. Park	9281
Exp Website	9152
BALANCE SHEET:	
Cash on hand	1001
Cash in bank	1002
Accounts Receivable	1060
Accounts Payable	2620
Inventory of goods for sale	1121
Computers, printers, etc. / CCA for this category	1773 / 1774
Other tangible assets; books, art, etc./ CCA for this category	1776 / 1777
Furniture: desk, filing cabinets, bookcases/ CCA for this category	1787 / 1788
Taxes payable, current year taxes owing, back taxes, HST	2680
Equity: Common shares	3500
Equity: Retained earnings	3600
Total Equity	3620

Total Assets	2599
Total Liabilities	3499

CCA Allowance

Capital Cost Allowance: What is it, how to claim it.

Capital cost allowance is a fancy way of saying "the maximum write-off per year".

The cost of depreciable assets, such as buildings, furniture and equipment, acquired for use in business or professional activities cannot be deducted as an up-front expense when calculating net income for tax purposes. In recognition, however, of the fact that these assets wear out or become obsolete over time and are replaced, the federal government created the capital cost allowance (CCA). The CCA is a non-refundable tax deduction that reduces taxes owed by permitting the cost of business-related assets to be deducted from income over a prescribed number of years.

- Cars, trucks, trailers and other motor vehicles are Class 10, written off at 30% of (last year's final total + new purchases*) per year.

IF purchased solely for business. OR if you buy a new car for $30k+ after 2000, they are class 10.1, solely for book-keeping. It makes no difference to the write-off amount.

- Computers, printers, copiers/ fax machines and office furniture are Class 8, written of at 20%/year.
- Computer programs are Class12, written off at 100%

because they upgrade so often.

These are really the only ones that apply as everything else is either a 100% deduction or goes into inventory, books purchased for sale, etc.

All of this goes onto form T-2125 if you file as a person, or in the T-2 form * if you file as a corporation. It's Form T-5013, schedule 8.

*The first you own a depreciable asset (car, desk, computer, etc) you can only write off 1/2 of the normal deduction for that item. For instance; a new car, normally written off at 30%/year is written of at 15% the year you buy it, and 30% every year thereafter. This affects only the new car, not everything I that class.

Use of Home/ Car

"Use of" Home and Car

You are expected to use a certain area of your home for writing, and to use your car for business.

You can claim either by square footage, more useful in a house with a lot of rooms, or by the number of rooms, which is more useful in a small apartment.

The math is easy; if you have a 2 bedroom apartment and you use one bedroom for your writing, then you simply add up the rooms (minus the bathroom). So 2 bedrooms, kitchen, dining and living rooms equals five rooms. You can write off 1/5 of your rent, hydro, heat, phone, internet, upkeep (repairs, painting, etc NOT new furniture of artwork).

Square footage is just a bit harder since you likely won't get a nice, round number like 20%.

Say you own a small house of 2200 square feet. You decide that the smallest bedroom will be your office. It's 9x10 or 90 square feet. 90/2200 equals 24.4 percent. If you do it by rooms; 3 bedrooms, kitchen, dining, living room, laundry room and finished basement... that's 1/8 or 12.5%.

Go with square feet.

Use of car is similar but more work.

You can either use the CRA approved standard of \$.54 for the first 5000 km, and \$.48 per km after that (applied only to business mileage) or calculate your actual expenses that year and divide by the fraction used for business.

In either case you MUST track your mileage. Get a special, small notebook just for this and keep it in the glove compartment. Or use some of the blank pages at the end of this book.

The simplest way is to detail only your business mileage. On Jan 1st, before you go anywhere, write down the current mileage on your car. This is used for both the final mileage of last year and the beginning mileage of this year.

Then write down the starting and finishing mileage of every business trip. On January 1st next year, write down the mileage again. This is your final mileage.

Calculate all of the kilometers used only for business. Calculate the total kilometers for the year. Calculate the percentage of km used for business out of total kilometers. It'll be similar to 3,455/22,180 equals 15.5%.

Now apply that percentage to all of your car expenses aside from parking. So; gas, oil, repairs, battery, insurance, car payment, etc.

Or use the actual number of kilometers used for business and multiply by the CRA approved amounts listed above. In this case; 3455 X $.54 equals $1865.70 is your vehicle deduction for the year.

CRA Links

Links to CRA Tax information:

T-1 Guide, return and schedules (Choose province)

http://www.cra-arc.gc.ca/formspubs/t1gnrl/menu-eng.html

Form T2125 Small Business explanations and requirements

http://www.cra-arc.gc.ca/E/pub/tg/rc4070/rc4070-e.html

Form T2125

http://www.cra-arc.gc.ca/E/pbg/tf/t2125/t2125-16e.pdf

Capital Cost Allowance, Schedule 8:

http://www.cra-arc.gc.ca/E/pbg/tf/t2sch8/t2sch8-14e.pdf

Balance sheet, Schedule 100

http://www.cra-arc.gc.ca/E/pbg/tf/t2sch100/t2sch100-14e.pdf

Income Statement, Schedule 125

http://www.cra-arc.gc.ca/E/pbg/tf/t2sch125/t2sch125-14e.pdf

Notes Checklist, Schedule 141

http://www.cra-arc.gc.ca/E/pbg/tf/t2sch141/t2sch141-14e.pdf

T-2 Before you start guide

http://www.cra-arc.gc.ca/E/pub/tg/t4012/t4012-02-e.html

T-2 Return (long form)

http://www.cra-arc.gc.ca/E/pbg/tf/t2/t2-16e.pdf

T-2 Return (short Form)

http://www.cra-arc.gc.ca/E/pbg/tf/t2short/t2short-16e.pdf

T-2 Schedules:

Capital Cost Allowance, Schedule 8:

http://www.cra-arc.gc.ca/E/pbg/tf/t2sch8/t2sch8-14e.pdf

Shareholder Information, Schedule 50

http://www.cra-arc.gc.ca/E/pbg/tf/t2sch50/t2sch50-06e.pdf

Balance sheet, Schedule 100

http://www.cra-arc.gc.ca/E/pbg/tf/t2sch100/t2sch100-14e.pdf

Income Statement, Schedule 125

http://www.cra-arc.gc.ca/E/pbg/tf/t2sch125/t2sch125-14e.pdf

Notes Checklist, Schedule 141

http://www.cra-arc.gc.ca/E/pbg/tf/t2sch141/t2sch141-14e.pdf

About the General Index of Financial Information

http://www.cra-arc.gc.ca/E/pub/tg/rc4088/rc4088-e.html

Complete list of GIFI codes

http://www.cra-arc.gc.ca/E/pub/tg/rc4088/rc4088-e.html#appendix_A

Endnotes

Notes:

There are a number of blank pages after this page. This is for you to take notes, list mileage or receipts, etc.

Everything in this book can be checked on https://www.canada.ca/en/revenue-agency/services/tax/businesses/small-businesses-self-employed-income.html or by calling 1-800-959-8182 for personal taxes and 1-800-959-5525 for business.

I charge $25/ hour to sit with you in private and discuss your particular situation, or explain the rules in simple language. You can contact me at my website email laurie@lauriestewart-author.com

NOTES AND RECEIPTS

NOTES!

NOTES!

NOTES!

NOTES!

NOTES!

NOTES!

NOTES!

NOTES!

NOTES!

NOTES!

NOTES!

NOTES!

NOTES!

NOTES!

NOTES!

Made in the USA
Monee, IL
04 November 2026

67375845R00059